W9-ALJ-213

Searchlight BOOKS™

Understanding the Coronavirus

# A Global Pandemic

Margaret J. Goldstein

Lerner Publications ◆ Minneapolis

Copyright © 2022 by Lerner Publishing Group, Inc.

All rights reserved. International copyright secured. No part of this book may be reproduced, stored in a retrieval system, or transmitted in any form or by any means—electronic, mechanical, photocopying, recording, or otherwise—without the prior written permission of Lerner Publishing Group, Inc., except for the inclusion of brief quotations in an acknowledged review.

Lerner Publications Company
An imprint of Lerner Publishing Group, Inc.
241 First Avenue North
Minneapolis, MN 55401 USA

For reading levels and more information, look up this title at www.lernerbooks.com.

Main body text set in Adrianna Regular.
Typeface provided by Chank.

**Library of Congress Cataloging-in-Publication Data**

Names: Goldstein, Margaret J., author.
Title: A global pandemic / Margaret J. Goldstein.
Description: Minneapolis, MN : Lerner Publications , [2022] | Series: Searchlight books - understanding the coronavirus | Includes bibliographical references and index. | Audience: Ages 8 –11 | Audience: Grades 10 –12 | Summary: "COVID-19 shocked the world in 2020. Follow the disease's spread across the globe and the different approaches countries took to fight back"— Provided by publisher.
Identifiers: LCCN 2021007536 (print) | LCCN 2021007537 (ebook) | ISBN 9781728428499 (library binding) | ISBN 9781728431468 (paperback) | ISBN 9781728430744 (ebook)
Subjects: LCSH: COVID-19 (Disease)—Juvenile literature. | COVID-19 (Disease)—Social aspects—Juvenile literature. | COVID-19 (Disease)—Government policy—Juvenile literature. | COVID-19 (Disease)—Treatment—Juvenile literature. | COVID-19 (Disease)—Prevention—Juvenile literature. | Epidemics—Juvenile literature. | Communicable diseases—Juvenile literature.
Classification: LCC RA644.C67 G6463 2022 (print) | LCC RA644.C67 (ebook) | DDC 362.1962/414—dc23

LC record available at https://lccn.loc.gov/2021007536
LC ebook record available at https://lccn.loc.gov/2021007537

Manufactured in the United States of America
1-49386-49490-4/26/2021

# Table of Contents

# Chapter 1

# BAD NEWS FROM CHINA

In late 2019, the Chinese government reported a new disease outbreak. Dozens of people in Wuhan, a city in central China, had gotten sick. Their symptoms included coughs, fevers, body aches, and trouble breathing. A new coronavirus was causing the illness.

In Wuhan, the virus began to spread. Chinese leaders feared it would spread to other cities in China and to other countries. They notified the World Health Organization (WHO), which is part of the United Nations.

## A Steady Spread

The new virus continued to spread. In China, more and more people got sick. Some of them died. International travelers carried the virus beyond China on airplanes, trains, and ships. On January 20, 2020, Japan, South Korea, and Thailand reported cases of the new virus. The next day, a US man was found to have the virus. He had been to Wuhan and returned to his home in Washington.

Over 11 million people live in Wuhan, China.

As the virus spread from country to country, the WHO declared a global health crisis. Medical researchers studied the virus. An international team of scientists gave it a name: SARS-CoV-2. News reporters referred to it as simply the coronavirus. The WHO named the disease caused by the coronavirus COVID-19.

COVID-19 affected people in different ways. Some infected people had no symptoms. Others had only mild symptoms. Some had trouble breathing and needed hospital care. Many of those patients died.

The WHO is based in Geneva, Switzerland.

# STEM Spotlight

Scientists think the coronavirus first infected bats in China. Bats spread the virus to other animals, which then passed it to people. But scientists aren't sure which animal or animals were the link between bats and humans. Scientists have explored several possibilities, including minks and ferrets, but they haven't yet found the answer. Whatever the animals were, people in China were infected when they interacted with them. Then the virus spread from person to person.

Chapter 2

# PUTTING ON THE BRAKES

As the virus spread around the world, governments tried to slow or stop it. China did not allow Wuhan residents to leave the city. The US government said that foreigners who had traveled in China could not enter the United States. Other nations restricted travel to and from China. Some countries closed their borders completely. But the virus continued to spread.

Scientists studied how the virus moved from person to person. They learned that when infected people sneezed, coughed, talked, or breathed, they released virus-filled droplets into the air. People standing nearby could inhale the droplets and become infected too.

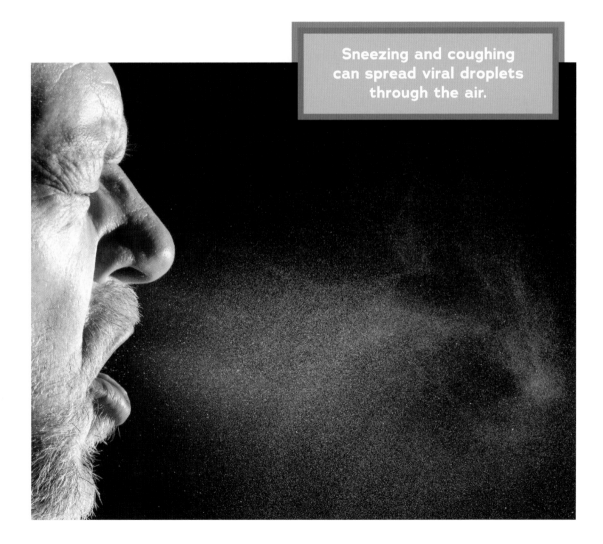

Sneezing and coughing can spread viral droplets through the air.

# Dr. Soumya Swaminathan

Dr. Soumya Swaminathan (*below*) is a physician. She studied medicine in India and the United States. She is an expert in respiratory diseases and has worked in the United States, Europe, and India. In 2017, she began working for the WHO. She became the WHO's chief scientist in 2019. When COVID-19 began to spread around the world, Swaminathan took the lead in educating people about vaccinations, quarantining, and other ways to keep people from getting sick.

Dr Soumya Swaminathan

WHO Chief Scientist

Government officials and medical professionals told people to wear face masks to stop the spread. Many nations required citizens to wear face masks in public. Other nations urged mask wearing but did not require it. Governments also recommended that people practice social distancing, or standing at least 6 feet (2 m) apart from one another.

People protect themselves and others by wearing masks in public.

# HEALTH WORKERS WEAR PROTECTIVE GEAR AS THEY TREAT PATIENTS.

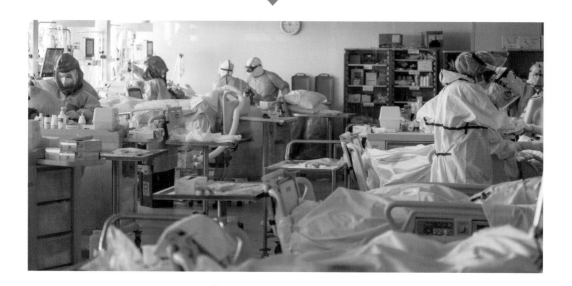

In March, the virus raged through Italy, Spain, and other parts of Europe. Thousands got sick. Hospitals filled up with patients, and doctors and nurses struggled to care for everyone. To keep people from infecting one another, many European nations temporarily closed restaurants, schools, factories, hotels, museums, movie theaters, gyms, and hair salons. They told people to stay home and avoid public gatherings. Many other nations, as well as some US states, also shut down businesses.

# Rules and Regulations

Governments took many steps to fight COVID-19. Public health agencies tested people to find out who had the coronavirus. Even people without symptoms can pass the virus to others. For that reason, anyone who tested positive was told to go into quarantine.

Mobile testing sites are used to help get people tested for COVID-19.

Some countries were very strict about quarantines. For instance, people who traveled to Hong Kong, a region in China, had to go into quarantine for two weeks. They wore electronic wristbands that tracked their movements. If someone left quarantine early, tracking software alerted the authorities. Other nations had few restrictions. For example, Mexico welcomed visitors with no requirements for quarantining.

A traveler is given a tracking wristband in Hong Kong.

# Chapter 3

# A TOUGH PROBLEM

As the pandemic swept around the world, it hit some countries harder than others. Most places saw waves of infection, with case numbers rising and falling several times. Using graphs and maps, epidemiologists tracked the virus.

Epidemiologists saw that strong government and community efforts helped in the fight against the coronavirus. For instance, when COVID-19 broke out in South Korea in February 2020, the nation took quick action. The government used contact tracing and quarantines to prevent further spread. South Korea didn't shut down businesses, but it implemented widespread testing. Citizens embraced mask wearing and social distancing. The effort paid off. The nation's COVID-19 case numbers dropped dramatically. By spring 2020, South Korea was reporting just a few new cases each day. International health leaders said the nation was a role model for virus control.

Wearing masks combined with social distancing has proved to be an effective way to control the spread of the virus.

THANK YOU FOR PRACTICING
**SOCIAL DISTANCING**

PLEASE KEEP AT LEAST 6FT APART

Many businesses use floor markings and signs to help people maintain social distancing.

As winter approached in South Korea, the weather grew colder. People spent more time indoors, where the virus spreads more easily. They wanted to gather with friends at parties, music clubs, and restaurants. These indoor gatherings increased South Korea's COVID-19 case numbers. In mid-December of 2020, the nation reported more than one thousand new cases per day.

The example of South Korea shows how hard it is to control the spread of the coronavirus. Other nations had similar experiences. They successfully kept the virus under control for many months only to see cases spike later on.

## PEOPLE CAN GET INFECTED WHEN THEY GATHER IN CROWDED PLACES, EVEN IF THEY WEAR MASKS.

▼

Some children do not have access to computers or reliable internet service, so they must attend school in person.

## Tailspin

The coronavirus was especially hard on communities experiencing poverty. Many people live in crowded homes and neighborhoods that make it difficult to social distance. People in these areas didn't have access to COVID-19 testing or contact tracing. Many people lacked proper medical care, nutrition, and sanitation to begin with. These factors put them at extra risk of dying from COVID-19.

Grocery workers are not able to do their jobs from home, so they are at higher risk of getting infected by the virus.

Around the world, unhoused people, migrants, refugees, and low-wage workers had similar problems staying safe and getting COVID-19 care. Many people also got sick on the job. In countries around the world, factory workers, bus drivers, grocery clerks, and farmworkers had to go to work. They risked infection in their workplaces because their jobs could not be done from their homes.

# Dr. Georges Bwelle

Dr. Georges Bwelle runs free health clinics in the African nation of Cameroon. During the pandemic, Bwelle changed his focus. He and his team of doctors, nurses, and volunteers assembled kits to help people in Cameroon stay safe from the coronavirus. The kits contained face masks and healthy food. Handwashing is important in the fight against COVID-19 since the coronavirus can live on the skin. So the kits also contained hand sanitizer and soap. In 2020, Bwelle and his team distributed more than 40,000 kits to people across Cameroon.

## Response of Leaders

Lack of specific guidelines from leaders also led to high COVID-19 numbers. For instance, the president of Brazil, Jair Bolsonaro, and the president of the United States, Donald Trump, did not call for nationwide restrictions to control the virus. They didn't follow advice from scientists and doctors about wearing masks.

Jair Bolsonaro is the president of Brazil.

President Joe Biden speaks about his COVID-19 plan in early 2021.

Without direction from leaders, some citizens also ignored medical advice. People gathered together without masks. This led to COVID-19 outbreaks in some US states. When Joe Biden became president of the United States in 2021, he vowed to make it a priority to fight COVID-19. He required people to wear masks while at federal government sites and offices and while traveling from one state to another. Biden asked all Americans to wear masks during his first 100 days in office. He pledged to distribute 100 million vaccines during that same time.

# Chapter 4

# HEALTH CARE FIGHTS BACK

Around the world, COVID-19 patients overwhelmed health care systems. Even in wealthy nations, hospitals didn't have enough staff, equipment, or beds to care for everyone who was sick.

Doctors knew that the best way to fight COVID-19 was to keep people from getting sick in the first place. That solution involved giving people a vaccine. Vaccines prepare the body's immune system to fight off certain viruses and bacteria. Drug companies worked to create a coronavirus vaccine. It was ready by late 2020.

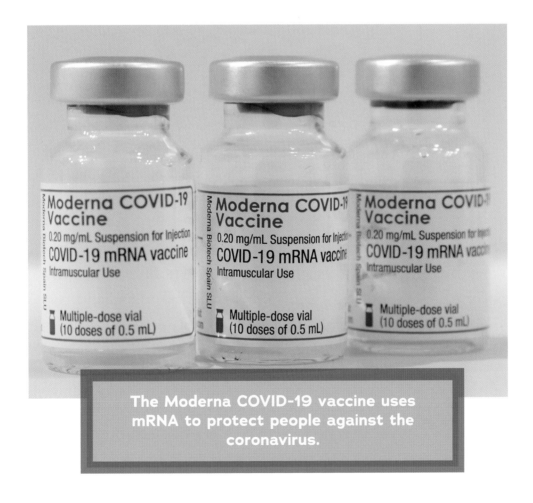

The Moderna COVID-19 vaccine uses mRNA to protect people against the coronavirus.

# VACCINES BUILD IMMUNITY AGAINST A VIRUS.

Widespread coronavirus vaccination will be a massive and lengthy job. Experts think it will take at least until the end of 2021 to vaccinate most of the people on Earth. Wealthy nations such as the United States have already purchased millions of vaccine doses. They are giving the vaccine first to essential workers and other vulnerable people, such as the elderly. Poor nations have less money for vaccine purchases and distribution. To address this inequality, the WHO and other health organizations created COVAX. It is an international effort to purchase vaccines and distribute them to people in nations that cannot afford to purchase vaccines for their citizens.

# STEM Spotlight

After COVID-19 vaccines are made, planes and trucks take them around the world to hospitals and pharmacies, where they are injected into patients. Transporting the vaccines is hard because they must be kept extremely cold or they will spoil. The vaccine from the drug company Moderna has to be kept at −4° F (−20°C). The vaccine from Pfizer must be kept at −94°F (−70°C). Keeping the proper temperatures all along the way requires special equipment, such as shipping boxes filled with dry ice, refrigerated trucks and vans, and super-cold freezers at vaccination centers.

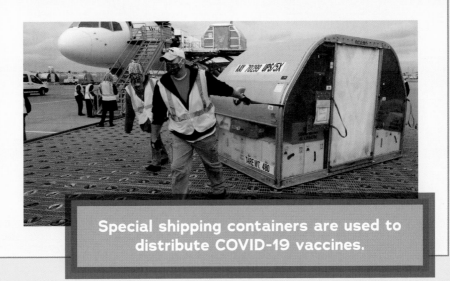

Special shipping containers are used to distribute COVID-19 vaccines.

## The Fight's Not Over

Widespread vaccination does not guarantee that COVID-19 will be gone for good. The coronavirus might continue to infect people for many years. It has begun to mutate, so new vaccines will need to be created to protect against new strains. Health experts say that other new viruses are likely to emerge in the future. When they do, people can use the lessons of COVID-19 to fight them. If we act quickly, we can control new disease outbreaks before they become pandemics.

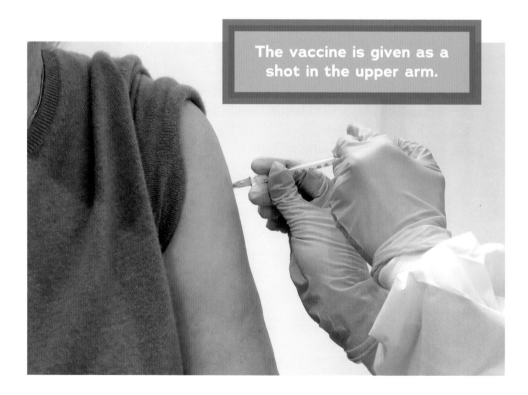

The vaccine is given as a shot in the upper arm.

# Important Dates

**December 2019**   Government officials in China report a new virus outbreak in the city of Wuhan.

**January 2020**   The virus is reported in countries outside of China.
The WHO declares the COVID-19 outbreak to be a global health emergency.

**April 2020**   The WHO and other health organizations create COVAX, a program to provide coronavirus vaccines to people in poor nations.

**September 2020**   The worldwide COVID-19 death toll reaches one million.

**December 2020**   A woman in the United Kingdom is the first person on Earth vaccinated for COVID-19.

**January 2021**   US president Joe Biden vows that 100 million Americans will be vaccinated during his first 100 days in office.

**February 2021**   Scientists identify new coronavirus variants in the United Kingdom, South Africa, and Brazil.

# Glossary

**coronavirus:** a virus whose surface is covered by spiky projections

**epidemiologist:** a scientist who studies disease outbreaks

**essential worker:** a person whose work is needed to keep society running

**immune system:** a network of cells, tissues, and proteins that defend the body against disease

**mutate:** to change over time

**pandemic:** a worldwide outbreak of a disease

**positive:** having an infection or illness, as indicated by a test result

**quarantine:** a specific time period during which people isolate themselves from others so as not to pass on a disease

**vaccine:** a substance that prepares the immune system to fight off an invader, such as a virus

**virus:** a tiny particle that can infect living cells and cause disease

# Learn More

Coronavirus: What Kids Can Do
   https://kidshealth.org/en/kids/coronavirus-kids.html?WT.ac=k-feat

COVID-19: Kids, Here's What You Need to Know
   https://www.canada.ca/en/public-health/services/diseases
   /coronavirus-disease-covid-19/resources-parents-children/kids-need
   -know.html

Gilles, Renae. *The Science of the Coronavirus*. Minneapolis: Lerner
   Publications, 2021.

Influenza Pandemic of 1918 Facts for Kids
   https://kids.kiddle.co/Influenza_pandemic_of_1918

Shoals, James. *Epidemics and Pandemics*. New York: Smartbook Media,
   2020.

Silver, Erin. *What Kids Did: Stories of Kindness and Invention in the Time
   of COVID-19*. Toronto: Second Story Press, 2020.

# Index

# Photo Acknowledgments

sleepingpanda/Shutterstock, p.5; EQRoy/Shutterstock, p.6; Martin Janca/Shutterstock, p.7; Rainer Fuhrmann/Shutterstock, p.9; REUTERS/Alamy, p.10; AS photostudio/Shutterstock, p.11; Michele Lapini/Stringer/Getty Images, p.12; Dan Kitwood/Staff/Getty Images, p.13; Anthony Kwan/Stringer/ Getty Images, p.14; Ezra Acayan / Stringer//Getty Images, p.16; Leland Bobbe/Getty Images, p.17; Alexandre Schneider/Stringer/Getty Images, p.18; Anindito Mukherjee/Stringer/Getty Images, p.19; Jacob Lund/Shutterstock, p.20; Kwame Amo/Shutterstock, p.21; Andressa Anholete/Stringer/Getty Images, p.22; Alex Won /Staff/Getty Images, p.23; Pool/Getty Images, p.25; Str/ZUMAPRESS/ Newscom, p.26; Pool/Getty Images, p.27; Pool/Getty Images, p.28

Cover: Cimmerian/Getty Images